Love
Taslir

Love Poems of Taslima Nasreen

TRANSLATED BY
Ashim Chowdhury

Rupa & Co

Copyright © Taslima Nasreen 2004
Translation copyright © Ashim Chowdhury 2004

Published 2004 by
Rupa & Co
7/16, Ansari Road, Daryaganj,
New Delhi 110 002

Sales Centres:
Allahabad Bangalore Chandigarh Chennai
Hyderabad Jaipur Kathmandu Kolkata
Ludhiana Mumbai Pune

All rights reserved.
No part of this publication may be reproduced, stored in a retrieval system, or transmitted, in any form or by any means, electronic, mechanical, photocopying, recording or otherwise, without the prior permission of the publishers.

The author asserts the moral right to
be identified as the author of this work.

Typeset in 12 pts Simoncini Garamond by
Nikita Overseas Pvt Ltd,
1410 Chiranjiv Tower,
43 Nehru Place,
New Delhi 110 019

Printed in India by
Rekha Printers Pvt Ltd,
A-102/1, Okhla Industrial Area,
Phase-II, New Delhi-110 020

Contents

Chastity	1
The outsiders	2
The musk of pain	3
The ledger	4
When I see you	6
The exile's poem	8
Exile	9
Calling a young man who's a home-bird	10
Castles in the air	11
Aftershave	12
Seascape	15
Thirty springs have gone by	17
Expectations	19
Delhi afternoons	20
Aloneness	23
I don't feel up to love these days	25
Obedience	26
Hope and despair	27

Giving	28
Body language	30
No matter, if he doesn't know	33
Immersion	34
Love	36
Somewhat like the ant	37
Talking letters	39
Fearless	41
Naya Paltan	42
Crazy talk	44
He will go	45
Pointless	46
Knowing	47
I never adjured you	48
Question	49
Love	50
Man — the word stirs me deeply	51
There is no age for love	53

Chastity

If a man touches my body
I'll become unchaste
and not if he touches my heart?
The heart lives freely
in the whole body.
I don't know who can get to the heart
without touching the body,
but I know it for sure
that human beings can't.

The outsiders

There are some
who never have a home,
a courtyard.

Sure, there are—
a city full of people,
yet no one to love them.

Aren't there some who grow old
looking at birds, sky,
men, forests,
sea and emptiness
all their lives?

And while growing old,
who, just before they die,
want some other life to live?

It isn't as if it never happens.
It does.

The musk of pain

Some wounds need no balm,
nobody's nursing;
staying up nights out of deep tenderness,
a change of air—
none of these:
they heal on their own.

Some pains burn you
all the time:
even the slight bodies of minor pains,
which the mouth can blow away—
carry the heat of fire.

These pains do not spear you
or make you go blind:
they only keep burning some things somewhere
and make them private embers.

Some pains dissolve in the air
before the night is out,
some pains set up home
in your heart
and, out of love, stay with you all your life.

The ledger

My day is never made
if I don't have a cup of ginger-tea in the morning.
In the operation theatre
I give some dying patients their medicines
after measuring them out,
try to decide if I should give them oxygen,
nitrous oxide, halothane and pethidine
in measured doses.
I take their pulses again and again,
their blood pressures.
I push saline into a left-hand vein,
if necessary, two pouches of blood
into the right hand too.
The whole afternoon goes like this.

If I can't do a round of the town
in the afternoon
I get the blues.
After listening to music in the evening,
or just gossiping,
or studying alone in my room,
when I hit the bed at midnight

all alone
I yearn for a hand to come and lift my chin
And a pair of lips to kiss my lips.

Without an intense kiss, my night is never made.

When I see you

When I see you
I want to begin my life
from the beginning.
When I see you
I want to die,
die and become sacred water
just on the off-chance
that you may touch it
if you're ever thirsty.

I'll give you my sky
you take sunshine, rains—
whatever and whenever you want;
I'll let my morphine spread over your sleeplessness.

Give me a night which is twelve years long
to see you.
You've outmooned the moon.
In your rays one day
I'll coil my hair into a pointed bun,
put vermillion on my forehead
and dress up to the nines to look a beauty.

When I see you
I want to die.
If your fire singes my mouth
when they cremate me,
I'll go to heaven.

The exile's poem

These days I often sit at the dining table
with fish and rice, take so much dal
that my wrist sinks into it, and mix;
my left hand swings from time to time
as if driving away flies.
In my airconditioned room in Scandinavia
there are absolutely no flies and bugs
and yet I fancy driving away something—
my grief?

The sad piece of fish, vegetables, the bit of salt
near the edge of the plate,
the rice mixed with the thick gravy—
I don't feel like taking my hand off the plate;
I feel like mixing rice like this the whole day
And eating it secretly.
I don't know why I want the taste and smell of rice so much,
preferring it to the golden spoon.
Actually, when I touch rice,
my hand doesn't bring up rice
but fistfuls of Bangladesh.

Exile

My country, how are you?
How are you, my country?
You, my country, how are you?
Are you keeping well, my country?

My heart yearns for you.
Don't you yearn for me?
My like is running out thinking of you,
and yours?
I die dreaming of you,
and you?

I hide my wounds in secret,
my sorrows
my tears;
hold back in secret
my unruly hair
flowers, sights.
I am not well,
you keep well, my beloved country.

Calling a young man who's a home-bird

Just come out into the yard,
I'll travel eleven thousand miles to meet you.
Just say my name once,
I'll pick all the gentians from the hilltop
and give them to you.
Just utter my name once
and I'll sprinkle on your body,
like the first rains of July,
all the colours of birch, maple and juniper trees.
Feel thirsty? Don't worry—
I'll give you alone
all the waters of the Danube, Seine, Tiber and Rhine.

Just come out into the yard,
I'll cross the longest sea and touch you.
Just say once that you love me,
then see if I don't snatch myself away
from this universe
and give myself to you.

Castles in the air

I wonder how you'd look lying down
or sleeping
how you'd look when you dreamed
when you woke from your dream
got up to go to the bathroom
had a glass of water from the jug—
I've never seen you in domestic life.
How would you look when you shaved,
when you had a bath,
and when you hummed a song?
(At bath, you generally prefer
to sing Tagore's songs or film songs maybe!)
I wonder how you'd look without your shirt on;
if somebody undid her forest of hair
on your wide chest and caressed it a lot;
when you suddenly woke up at dead of night
and drowned yourself in the waves of a woman-river
in a fit of wild love-making.

I'm dying to see one day
how a woman's body thrills
when your fingers touch it.

I want so much to be a woman once!

Aftershave

You smell of aftershave—
whether the smell is French or English
I cannot guess.
When I kiss you
I'll put my lips on your aftershaved forehead, cheeks, throat;
the music of your aftershaved button being yanked
makes me wet with happiness, makes me wet;
the day I yank out your button
I feel good.

You use so much aftershave
that I feel drunk
when I put my face on your chest.
So much aftershave that like a creeper
I twist and turn and do something so crazy
that I don't know how many times
you mentally tell me off – daredevil rogue.

Without aftershave you're like a brick,
A log of wood or stone.
Then I don't feel like touching you or anything.
I don't feel up to a bath,

my body doesn't play like a sitar
if your hair smells of hair
your arms of flesh and your fingers of bones alone,
I bring up blood.

Do I love your aftershaved smell
More than you? I wonder.
If another man comes after a bathe in a river of scent
Why, I don't even feel like touching him.

Seascape

I was also eighteen once;
the sea called all night
in my sleep.
At eighteen everybody hears the lapping of the sea
within and without.

Now the body is too wave-bitten,
now the salt of the sea tastes like scales of fish,
now I put up the dam of life
to push back the tide.

Eighteen doesn't take a long time to end.
The tide comes, the tide-swept people call,
the birds call, the way calls,
the anxious hands of the traveler—
we do not know when we cross "under thirty."

The waters of life collect
become so vast
so endless
that, if you compare the two,
the sea seems like a lake in the afternoon.

16 • LOVE POEMS OF TASLIMA NASREEN

Thirty springs have gone by

Thirty springs have gone by
falling in love with the wrong men,
and yet, even now,
the heart seems to ache—
even now when the deceiving males
touch my fingers
a waterfall cascades down my rock-body.

Now I seem to hear something like the babble of water
in lonely summer, winter, spring—
thirty springs have gone by
falling in love with the wrong men,
yet I burn myself to a cinder
in the sunshine of faith.

If the deceiving males call even once
I forget the tears of the past,
forget the cloudy skies, the never-ending nights,
forget all and rush into new mistakes.
If a man loves me even once
I forget everything and start crying like an innocent
  young girl.

Thirty years have gone by
falling in love with the wrong men;
a thousand more years will go by,
but the stupid girl will never learn her lesson.

Expectations

You've given him everything ungrudgingly,
you thought he too would give you something in return.
No way. You remain alone with emptiness
and he quickly runs far away.
It's a mistake to expect anything in return
when you love.

You've lost the lighted room
and grasped the wooden post of darkness.
Those who go, go away laughing.
They never look back.
You're given everything—to the last morsel—
though you've got nothing in return.
You go hungry, but they gorge on your wealth—
the people you've loved
squeezing yourself dry.
You'll be in for a let down for sure
if you love and secretly expect
something in return — even love.

Delhi afternoons

So many afternoons come
but nothing like those afternoons of joy
in New Delhi.
I long to go there again and see
if the rooms are still as they were,
if, when you stand in the lobby,
You can still touch the sky.
Does anybody, all on a sudden,
still burst into song in the afternoon
out of love, just like that?

I long to go again and see
if they are still as they were:
the India Gate in the evening,
the water and the grass, bhelpuri;
see if at the Old Fort,
on the footpath, at Palika Bazar—
anybody kisses somebody like that,
not giving a hoot about who's watching.

I long to go out again,
Wearing long shorts and a sleeveless vest,

to enjoy the early evening breeze
and to see if the bathtub, the bed
and the pillows
are still in their places.

Afternoons still come.
But is there a single afternoon like those?

Aloneness

I go wherever my eyes take me.
Who'll come and stand
like a rock before me
and stretch out his hands?
There are so many diseases in my heart,
Who'll cure them?

I don't feel up to love these days

I don't feel up to love these days.
It seems as if there's some work to be done,
as if I'm supposed to go somewhere,
somewhere far away.
Love doesn't string me like a necklace any more these days
as the long string of pain does.

My heart aches for these who live
as if they're dead.
If it aches all day,
and needles poke me,
am I mad that I'll leap at love?
First I'll have to help those who're floating,
first I'll have to stretch my hand
towards those who're drowning.
After that, if I live, I'll live,
if I love, I'll love.

Obedience

If you say, "Come," I come.
If you say, "Go," I go.
Whether I get anything or not,
I dance day and night
To your time.
Tell me, do I live for myself?

Hope and despair

So many things ring;
every pore of the body;
the mind rings and rings;
dancing seven times round the courtyard of the mind,
the tinkling anklet rings alone;
the silver bangles studding the hands
jingle and ring.
The windowpane rings
to the drumming of the monsoon rains;
thunder rings
as clouds clash against each other;
dreams ring to three-beat music;
aloneness rings in the morning
in a wild frenzy.

So many things ring,
only the doorbell never does.

Giving

Beg, just once.
This is *my* hand : it can never give pennies.
If I have to give you something,
I'll give you gold coins.

Knock on the door and stand and wait, beggar,
knock, knock,
break my million-year sleep once
if you can.
These are *my* eyes—
is there any sky bluer than these?
Have no fear. I'll give you gold coins.

Beg. Ask and see:
no matter what I can do
I can never refuse anyone
once they put out their hands.

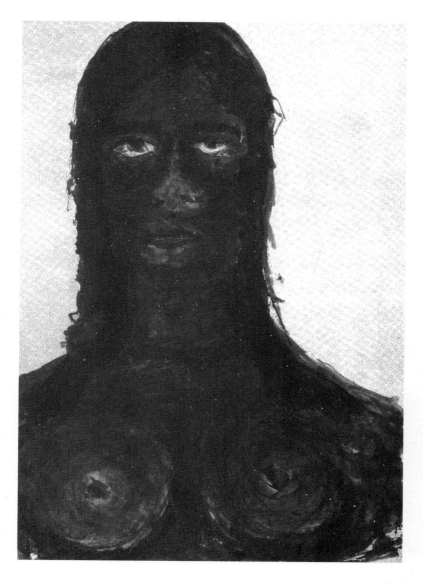

Body language

I've known my body for so long,
yet sometimes I don't know it myself.
If a rough hand
contrives to touch my hand
painted with sandal-paste,
a bell rings and rings
in the belfry of my nerves.

It's my own body
but I can't read its language.
It speaks on its own,
in its own language.
Then my fingers, eyes, these lips,
these smooth legs
aren't mine any more.

These hands are mine
and yet I don't know them properly;
these are my lips, my breasts,
thighs, shanks—
but not one of their muscles or pores
is under my control.

The bell rings
in the belfry of my nerves.
Then, whose plaything am I in this world—
man's or nature's?

Actually,
it's nature, not man, who plays me.
I'm her fancy sitar.

A man's touch wakes me up
from my childhood sleep.
Suddenly, my sea is in tide.
If she smells the fragrance of love
in my flesh and blood,
it's nature who plays me.
I'm her fancy sitar.

No matter, if he doesn't know

Does he know
that even now I remember him,
want him?
That even now
I warm my body at midnight
in the fire of his memories?

If he doesn't know,
what does it matter?
This is my happiness:
that I love him
whether he loves me or not.

Immersion

"Let's go near the river,"
I say to him.
He shrugs, his eyes indifferent yet tender,
and says, "Let's."
—"You like the river a lot, don't you?"
I say, "An awful lot."
The river is a lot like my faraway childhood.
I can see its banks and yet
if I stretch my hand
I cannot touch it—only sigh.

He walks by my side and says:
"You also like the moon, don't you?"
I say, "I do. A lot."
—"And the autumn breeze?"
—"That too"
—"Well, during the full moon,
in the forest,
the smell of unknown flowers,
you're absolutely alone—
don't you feel a bit scared?"
An ecstasy I can't describe

thrills my body and mind.
"Scared of what?" I say. "Ghosts?"
—"No, scared of me!"

Then, laughing, he touches my warm palm.
By this time we've come
quite close to the river
I'm drunk on his touch, smell—
suddenly he gives me a shove
towards the swift current.
I stumble into the churning,
hungry, gaping mouth of the water,
sink and float again,
and he laughs standing on the bank.
Does anybody know it better than him
that I can't swim?

I love him.
Let this alone be my sin or grace.
Let this alone be my happiness.
Or my heart's grief.

Love

If somebody loves you
just roasted brinjal
and rice
mashed with a couple of green chillies,
the night spent on the footpath
—yet you feel a different joy of victory.

If somebody loves you,
you can take life
between your two fingers
and nicely smoke it away;
a magic sitar without strings
starts playing in your heart.

Somewhat like the ant

If we meet twice a year
face to face like that
we won't touch each other:
just say "How's life?" and a couple of things like that;
memory will shake its branches like mad
in the blood.
A heap of happiness
will raise a storm in the tears.

You'll talk of love at random and
your vegetable soup will get cold on the table;
looking at your eyes,
at your tongue in tide
I'll long so much to live!

If we meet at least once a year
and, incidentally, you also talk of love,
water will suddenly cataract into the drought of my life.

If we don't meet even once a year
I'll still think you love me—even though it isn't true.
An ant can live without love,
but a human being?

The straight road

If you want to fall in love with me, do.
I've put out my well-rounded hands, see.
If you want to hold them, do.

I've no time to stand on the road.
If I have to pull in my hands,
if we can't agree,
get out of my way.

Talking letters

These days I have started standing out again
in the morning, after opening the door.
But not to dry my hair.
The peanut wallah goes this way
late in the afternoon,
and as for the chirping of birds
that can be heard better
from inside the house
The boris dry in the sun on the terrace*.
To see young men with well-groomed hair —
I'm not that young any more.
Then?

To tell the truth, I've picked up a new bad habit.
The postman goes this way
in the morning;
if by chance he delivers a letter,
the kids of the house may unwittingly
make it into an airplane and play with it.

---

* pulse-paste globs which are dried in the sun and cooked with vegetables

It is this fear
that prompts me to come out.

Not that it doesn't cross my mind at all:
You're quite busy living with your family,
watering the woodrose plant
late in the afternoon,
going out for a stroll in the evening
with your wife and kids—
Why should you write letters?
Do people write to anyone when they're happy?

Fearless

What shall I fear
when you've said you're there?
Whether you're there or not,
because I'm deaf and was born blind,
I'll know that somebody is standing by my side.
Imagining that my five fingers
are on his shoulder
I can go anywhere
without any hesitation.
Because you've said out of love
you're there.

Naya Paltan

At the crossing of Naya Paltan I'll meet him.
You know who? A handsome young man.
When I look at him,
like the banks of a river,
like Pompeii caving in after the eruption,
like the rain of ice
that falls in winter in Siberia,
I too break and fall
like tiny flakes of snow.

The young man doesn't even turn around
to look at me.
He has no time for other people's grief.
Still I go to Naya Paltan every day.
You know why?
Just on the off-chance
that I'll find him there
and he'll turn around
to look at me!

Crazy talk

One day I'll go build a house by the sea.
Sometimes I want to build it near the mountains.

If the fog of emptiness
drips from the sky of such solitary exile,
I will get soaked through and through
in the endless waters,
come in for fever and shiver.
Do come, even if not to see me.
People come even to see illness, don't they?

He will go

The dream comes from the south-west
every day
wearing a gray shirt,
says a few medium-sized words
and goes away.
He doesn't sit anywhere for long.
I ask him how he is.
He shakes his first finger
and makes a dewdrop or two
fall from the rose petals.

He wets his hand in the dew
and runs away, stealthily scaling the wall.
There has been a police circular about him
for the last eighteen years.
The dream will leave town today
and run away to the north at midnight.
I've heard that he'll go to the forest now.

Pointless

The man I'm waiting for
is not a friend, relation or neighbour —
nothing of the kind.
It isn't as if
the man I'm waiting for
will surely come.

Still I wait
because I've no crutches to help me get up,
no known way, no different sky,
because I've no life to live.

This waiting is absolutely pointless.
This warmth of sitting and waiting,
swinging with bated breath in hope—
has it any meaning at all?
How stupid women are:
they want so much to live with some false dreams!

Knowing

He isn't that much a male
As I thought:
Half of him is neuter
Half male.

You spend a whole life with a man
Sit and sleep with him
But how much do you know the real man?
All these days I thought I'd correctly sized him up,
but he isn't like that at all;
the man I think I know is the man
I don't know the most.

He isn't that much a man
as I thought:
He's half a beast
Half a man.

I never adjured you

You say so many times that you love me
that sometimes I make the mistake of believing
that you really do.
I should have known
that if somebody keeps saying something non-stop,
it doesn't become true.
Love isn't a mere word,
love is being absorbed—sacrifice.
How absorbed are you?

I never adjured you that you must love me.
Don't love me. A thousand people don't love me.
Have I died because of that?
Don't love me—that's much better,
but don't drown and choke me
in a sea of lies.

Question

Can you give something
better than love?
A sword which is sharper than
me?

Love

The years fall off
the branches of my life.
Still love blooms in the heart
unrestrained . . .
The Baltic Sea has no tides.
But see, sitting on its shore,
my whole body is in tide.

Man — *the word stirs me deeply*

Yes, the word stirs me.
I can't live in a forest where there are no men;
even in a silent room, if there are no people in it,
I get goosebumps.
I was gladder to see people than the sea
on St. Martin Island.
Man is more beautiful than the sunrise over the
Kanchenjunga,
more beautiful than the sky-scraping mountains of Kashmir,
man is much taller than the tall buildings in Manhattan.
The waterfall of love in a man's heart
moves me more than the Niagra.
Man—the word deeply stirs me.
Mountain peaks, flowers, butterflies, rivers or seas,
Buildings, diamonds, gold, jungles —
nothing draws me so much
as man draws me.
Nothing devours me
and floods me so much as man.

Man . . . I have not come across a more beautiful word.

There is no age for love

Is there any rule that you can fall in love
only if you are twenty-twenty-five?
There is no age for love, silly.
The undercurrent of love can flow
even at sixty
as it can at sixteen.

Even at sixty
the heart can cry a lot,
the love-thirsty fingers can shake
when you embrace somebody.
Even at sixty,
there can be a surge
in your heart.
The desire to pick the lotus
after scouring the mud
does not die.

Age is an insignificant string
you can jump over if you want.
As you get older
the plant of love grows by leaps and bounds

till it becomes a tree and touches the sky.
Take it from me, the more you age,
the more you love.